# NEPTUNE'S POOLS
Lune poems about the ocean

Published by SAKURA BOOK PUBLISHING
- South Africa
alta@sakurabookpublishing.com

**978-0-6398518-6-0 Paperback**
**978-0-6398518-7-7 eBook**

All rights reserved. No part of this publication may be reproduced, stored in a retrieval system, or transmitted in any form by any means electronic, mechanical, photocopying, recording or otherwise without the written permission of the copyright owner.

© Charles R Haffner 2025
© Alta H Haffner 2025

# ABOUT THE AUTHORS

Charles R Haffner Was born in Baltimore Maryland and lived in Central Florida for 15 years. For the past two years, he has written 13 books consisting of various forms of micro poetry. His books can be found on amazon.com and he is the co-owner of Sakura Book Publishing. He resides in South Africa.

Alta H. Haffner is a Haiku poet whose work captures the essence of precious, fleeting moments with simplicity and depth. Born with a deep appreciation for the beauty of brevity, Alta's Haiku poems reflect her keen observation of nature and her ability to evoke emotions in just a few short lines.
Drawing inspiration from the ever changing seasons, the delicate balance of the natural world, and the quiet whispers of every new dawn, Alta's Haiku poems invite readers to slow down, pause, and appreciate the present moment. With a handful of syllables, she allows her readers to contemplate. Through her Haiku poetry, Alta H. Haffner reminds us of the beauty that can be found in simplicity, the power of mindfulness, and the importance of being fully present in

Bright azure sky light
reflections of puffy clouds
chilled white mountain peaks
Waters reflecting this love
In  syllables of  poems.

Ocean breeze in our hair. Sandy toes walking along the beaches in our hearts. From oceans to the seven seas, we present the love, humor, and darkness of each known memory. They say water represents life, but I think it symbolizes all of the senses and emotions. A moment of peace or a storm in my heart. I want to share everything with only you.

**Sharing emotions pieces of me watered down ocean's poetry.**

The deep ocean blue
meditate
reflecting my peace.

Negativity
waves crashing
tears fall with dawns light.

Azure skies above
inner peace
seagulls greet at dawn.

Bluish green water
my heart thumps
as sharks swim closer.

Dark night wind chills
sound of waves
warm feet in the sand.

Lovers in moonlight
embraced now
promises to stars.

Natural painting
Calming sea
strokes of blue and green.

Captivated hearts
I love you
breathing in the waves.

Blue kaleidoscope
sleepless waves
to dancing seagulls.

Daily dolphin dance
pretty screen
any sailors dream.

Serenade at dusk
seagulls feast
playful teasing breeze.

Pearly seashells shine
crushing waves
tangerine 'morn skies.

Evening dark shadows
breeze blowing
just the moon smiling.

Echos of the waves
lulling noise
memories collide.

Treasured moments speak
salted words
pouring from the sea.

Silence between stars
dull half-moon rising slowly
the sound of seagulls.

Waves hugging the shore
emotions
droplets kiss the sand.

Tranquility held
quiet mind
endless peace and hope.

Deadliest midnight
canoe floats
moonlit scary sea.

Ocean breathes in deep reflection
sun simmer down slow.

Magnificence felt embrace life romantic tango .

Following them all
humpbacks sing
an ocean of tears.

Seaweed swirling 'round
shimmering
heartbeat, sudden pause.

The sound of the breeze
take it in
inhale nature's gift.

Calm breeze today sings
sailboat sighs
Ocean's lullaby.

Merge with pale sunsets
soul within
moon keeps my secrets.

Hand in hand we walk
the warm sand
only cold waves left.

Breeze of the ocean
salty waves
I await the moon.

Morning walks footprints
meditate
soaking in the sun.

Choppy waves beckon
calling me
marine dance in spring.

Coral reefs broken
like our dreams
they repair with time.

Bluewater splashing
printed steps
one step at a time.

Chapters of my life memories
Ocean of my thoughts.

To listen closely
whispering
ocean sounds of love.

Ocean of nightmares?
peaceful dream?
listen sirens sing.

For the love I feel
reefs bottom
floating on love now.

Moon shines overhead
waves roll in
ocean's doorway sings.

Listen to the sounds
breathing in
breathing out at last.

My blue colored dreams
stretching far
as a lovely sea.

Smiling everyday
as the waves
sweep me off my feet.

Loving me each day
blue waters
calling only me.

The bluest waters
with such waves
postal cards in shops.

Distant whales singing
audience
of many birds clap.

Cooling myself in
calm waters
floating and so free.

Give me life today
as the waves
show me the way home.

Indian Ocean
blue waters
in my Durban dream.

Kissing my cold lips
bringing life
a marine in dreams.

Seagulls flapping their
tired wings
on an ocean beach .

Tiny tears spilling
from the eyes
an ocean of guilt.

Sand covered beaches
in front of
ocean filled dreamers.

Painting the skyline
on wet sands
colorful love sketch.

Jet skis riding by
laughing teens
dating on the waves.

Summer storms brewing
clouds hover
over the boardwalk.

Black light with a haze
smoke rises
wave machine clicking.

Holding your soft hands
along our
favorite beaches.

Lovers wading through
summer blues
sea of our kisses.

Crab nets are ready
some buckets
empty some are full.

Forget the world now
absorb the
feelings on the sands.

A bride and groom wait
by the sea,
a wet ceremony.

Collecting sea shells
many echos
final pain released.

Distant clouds appear
cargo ship
on the horizon.

Our happy place is
is always
an ocean away.

Fisherman bluffs the
lone swordfish
with buckets of chum.

Beautiful sunsets
over seas
fiery skies and blue

Hints from salty winds
mixing up
in a lovely brew.

Slow drops of rain pour
over an
ocean of our truth.

Water skiing in the future African ocean.

Treasured waters sing
many tales
pirates exploring.

I painfully wait
by the sea
hoping to see you.

Dragging in water
spotted gown
sea of solitude.

Fishing in the sea
charter boat
of many tourists.

Rainbow colored sky beautiful moments on the sea.

Such tender moments
while in love
kissing on the beach.

Dolphins racing by
a cruise ship
watch the children smile.

Tales of mermaids,
rum barrels
of such ocean blues.

Desperate snow falling
across seas
feeling rejected.

Slight pings on sonar
schools of fish
escape in the dark sea.

Loving my Alta
in every
ocean that I dream.

Missing the waters
of my home
where your heart does roam.

Sharks in the water
drunk captain
capsized our old boat.

Parasailing on
our ocean
flying in this  love.

Nets in the water
fog rising
fishermen return.

Burial at sea
flagged casket
mourning our lost love.

Give me the smiles I
dream about
love me at the sea.

Cursed waters bring
the tears of
sailors when drowning.

Chasing the boats that
bring me love
in our ocean's spray.

Foundation of our love, always will be any beach.

Moon shining so bright
over waves
of our ocean's night.

Swimming in your heart
hold me tight
before love coasts away.

# Moon's reflection on a dark sea sailor's diary.

Cloudy days spoil all
sunbathers
so irritating.

Colorful kites fill
summer skies
over children's beach.

Moonlit channel a
tugboat sails
with an ocean breeze.

Ocean's waters bring
hidden truth
in the calmest waves.

Balloon of our hope
slowly floats
ocean's destiny.

Holding on a raft
fearful of
drowning in sorrow.

Ocean's kisses brings happiness
riding many waves.

www.ingramcontent.com/pod-product-compliance
Lightning Source LLC
Chambersburg PA
CBHW062052290426
44109CB00027B/2807